Home Into Trust Made Easy

Move Your House into a Trust, Avoid Probate, and Do It for Under £400 / $600

Jim Steve Garner

ISBN: 978-1-7642608-9-3

Disclaimer

This book explains in plain language how homeowners in the **United Kingdom** and the **United States** can move their property into a trust without spending thousands on legal fees. It is designed for **educational purposes only**.

It does **not provide legal, financial, or tax advice**. Laws and procedures vary by state, county, or region, and they may change over time. Always verify with your **mortgage lender**, **HM Land Registry (UK)**, or **County Recorder (US)** before making any transfer. Consult a qualified solicitor, attorney, or tax professional if your situation involves:

- High-value estates
- Blended families
- Rental or business properties
- Vulnerable beneficiaries
- Complex inheritance disputes

Case examples used in this book are composites and intended only to illustrate key points. Any resemblance to actual people or events is purely coincidental.

By reading this book, you agree that the author and publisher are **not responsible for any outcomes**—financial, legal, or otherwise—resulting from the use of its contents

Table of Contents

Preface

Most people think moving their home into a trust is something only wealthy families or lawyers can do. That's not true. The process is often made to look complicated, but in reality, with the right guidance, you can do it yourself for a fraction of the cost.

This book was written for everyday homeowners — people like you who simply want to protect their family, save money, and avoid legal headaches later on. You don't need a law degree. You don't need to spend thousands. What you need are clear, simple steps and a bit of confidence.

For many of us, a home is more than just bricks and mortar. It's the place filled with memories, family dinners, laughter, and sometimes even tears. It's where we've built our lives. That's why protecting it matters so much.

Too often, people put this kind of planning off, thinking everything will sort itself out later. But the truth is, without the right preparation, your family could face court delays, heavy fees, or even disagreements when you're no longer here. A trust is one of the most reliable ways to prevent that.

The problem is that most guides out there are either written in legal jargon no one understands or designed to push you toward hiring expensive lawyers. This book is different. It speaks directly to you, in plain words, with step-by-step instructions you can actually follow.

Here's what you'll discover:

- **How to save money.** You'll see how this can be done for a few hundred pounds or dollars, not thousands.

- **How to save time.** Your family won't be stuck waiting for courts or piles of paperwork.
- **How to save stress.** You'll gain peace of mind knowing your home is already protected.

The truth is simple: this book matters because your family matters. And you deserve to have the knowledge and confidence to make the right choices without breaking the bank.

As you turn these pages, keep this in mind — this isn't just about property. It's about security, dignity, and love for the people who mean the most to you. You can do this. Let's begin.

Jim Steve Garner

Introduction

Why people think trusts are complicated and expensive

If you've ever asked a solicitor in the UK or an estate planning attorney in the US about putting your house into a trust, chances are you were quoted a fee that made your jaw drop. We're talking £1,500 to £3,000 in the UK, or $2,000 to $5,000 in the US. And that's just for the paperwork. Many professionals give the impression that trusts are some mysterious, locked-away process that only they can manage. The truth? The legal world has a habit of dressing simple tools in heavy robes of jargon.

The average person hears words like "discretionary," "irrevocable," "appointment of trustees," or "alienation clause" and immediately feels out of their depth. Add in talk of inheritance tax, capital gains, and probate, and it's no wonder people back away. A woman in Bristol once told me she felt like she needed a law degree just to ask the right questions. In Chicago, a father said his attorney handed him a trust packet "thicker than a phone book" and still couldn't give a clear yes or no about selling his house later. Sound familiar?

That confusion, combined with the heavy costs, keeps many homeowners from even considering trusts. And yet, most of the so-called complexity boils down to two or three forms, one notarisation or ID check, and a signed deed. That's it. The rest is professional padding.

The truth: you can do it legally and safely for a few hundred

Now, here's the thing. Putting a house into a trust is not free. There are fees you cannot avoid — Land Registry in the UK, county recording fees in the US, identity verification, maybe a notary. But those fees are modest. In the UK, a full transfer with mortgage consent can be completed for under £400. In the US, most counties charge between $50 and $250 to record a new deed, plus the cost of notarisation. Add the small extras, and you're still well under $600.

Does this mean everyone should rush to DIY without a second thought? Not exactly. There are still rules to follow: lender consent, correct execution of the deed, correct witnessing. But with a step-by-step guide in plain language, you don't need to spend thousands. This book is built around one simple principle: ordinary people can set up a trust legally, safely, and affordably.

Who this book is for

This book is written for homeowners — not lawyers, not tax professionals, not trust corporations. If you own a home in the UK or US and have ever thought, *I want my kids to inherit smoothly without legal chaos,* this is for you. If you're worried about the mortgage lender calling in your loan, or about whether you'll lose control once the trust is in place, you're in the right place.

It's also for people who feel intimidated by formal legal writing. You won't find walls of technical text here. Instead, you'll find plain talk. For example, I'll explain the Trusts of Land and Appointment of Trustees Act 1996 in the UK without making you feel like you've stepped into law school. I'll break down the Garn–St. Germain Act of 1982 in the US without pages of cross-referencing.

If you're the kind of person who likes ticking boxes, following a checklist, and getting things done without overpaying, you'll feel at home here. And if you're the kind of person who has been putting this off for years because it felt too hard, this book will finally make it doable.

What you'll learn step by step

By the time you reach the end, you'll know exactly how to:

- Choose the right type of trust for your situation (life interest, discretionary, or revocable living trust).
- Talk to your lender and get written consent without tripping over technical terms.
- Draft a trust deed that actually holds up, even if you're the only trustee.
- Fill in the key forms — TR1, AP1, and ID1 in the UK; quitclaim or warranty deed in the US.
- Submit your paperwork correctly and avoid rejection.
- Keep your insurance valid and your mortgage secure.
- Understand how selling works once the property is in a trust.
- Avoid common mistakes that trip up most DIYers.

You'll also learn how to keep the entire process under £400 in the UK or $600 in the US. Along the way, you'll see real examples — like Sarah from Manchester, who set up a trust for her semi-detached without a solicitor, and James from Ohio, who recorded a quitclaim deed for $110 and walked out of the county recorder's office relieved that it wasn't rocket science after all.

Key takeaways from the introduction

- Most people think trusts are complicated because professionals frame them that way.

- The real process is far simpler: it's about deeds, consent, and registration.
- You don't need to spend thousands; the true cost is a few hundred.
- This guide is for ordinary homeowners in the UK and US who want control and clarity.
- By the end, you'll know how to complete the process legally and affordably, step by step.

Chapter 1 – What a Trust Really Is

Why the word "trust" throws people off

Say the word "trust" out loud. What's the first thing that comes to mind? For some people, it's old family money — the "trust fund kids" stereotype. For others, it's a mental image of dusty legal books and lawyers in dark suits billing by the hour. For most, it's confusion. "A trust… isn't that only for the rich?" or "Doesn't that mean I give up control of my house?"

The funny thing is, a trust is one of the simplest legal ideas ever invented. It's not magic, and it's not limited to wealthy families. At its heart, a trust is just an agreement about who looks after something and who gets to benefit from it. That's all. If you've ever asked a neighbor to hold a spare set of your keys "just in case," you've basically created a mini-trust: you remain the owner of the house, your neighbor holds the keys (like a trustee), and your family benefits if they need to get inside.

So why does it feel so complicated when lawyers explain it? Because they wrap it in language that sounds intimidating. Words like "settlor," "discretionary," "revocable," "equitable interests" — they scare off the average person. But the idea itself is straightforward. You put something (like a house) into a trust, a trustee looks after it, and the beneficiaries benefit.

The three roles that make up every trust

Think of a trust as a play with three main characters. Without them, the story doesn't work.

1. **The Settlor**
   - This is the person who sets up the trust. In most cases, that's you, the homeowner.
   - You decide the rules, you decide who benefits, and you decide who manages it.
   - In the UK, the term "settlor" is standard. In the US, you'll often hear "grantor" or "trustor." Same idea, different word.
2. **The Trustee**
   - This is the person (or people) who hold legal title to the property.
   - Their job is to follow the rules you set in the trust deed.
   - In many cases, the settlor and trustee are the same person. Yes, you can be both. That way, you don't give up control.
   - Example: In the US, Sarah sets up a revocable living trust, names herself trustee, and keeps running her home just as before.
3. **The Beneficiaries**
   - These are the people who benefit from the property in the trust.
   - Usually, they're your children, your spouse, or whoever you want to inherit smoothly.
   - They don't control the property while you're alive, but they get the benefit later.

That's it. One person sets it up, someone (maybe the same person) manages it, and someone benefits.

How the UK sees trusts

In the UK, trusts are deeply rooted in history. They go back to medieval times when knights went off to battle and needed someone to manage their land for their families. That's where the Trusts of Land and Appointment of Trustees Act 1996 (TOLATA) comes into play today — the modern rules that govern trusts holding property.

For property, the most common types are:

- **Life Interest Trust** – lets someone (usually a spouse or partner) live in the property for life, but ensures it eventually passes to children.
- **Discretionary Trust** – the trustee decides when and how to benefit the named people. Good for families who want flexibility.
- **Bare Trust** – property is held for someone outright (common for children).

Case example: Margaret, a widow in Manchester, wanted her second husband to stay in her home if she died, but she also wanted to guarantee her two sons from her first marriage would eventually inherit. A solicitor quoted her £2,200 to draft a life interest trust. Using simple forms and a clear trust deed, she did it herself for under £350. The Land Registry updated the title, Santander confirmed their charge stayed, and her sons had peace of mind.

How the US sees trusts

In the US, trusts are part of everyday estate planning, especially the **revocable living trust**. This trust is used to keep property out of probate court (the slow, expensive process that happens when someone dies).

The two most common types:

- **Revocable Living Trust** – you create it, you control it, you can cancel it. Best for homeowners who want control during life and a smooth handover after death.
- **Irrevocable Trust** – can't be changed easily. Used for asset protection or tax planning. Most people don't need this for their house.

Case example: James, a father in Ohio, had one goal — make sure his two daughters got his house without probate. His attorney quoted him $3,000 for a trust package. Instead, he used a standard revocable living trust template, signed it with witnesses, filed a quitclaim deed at the county recorder's office for $110, and walked out with the property safely titled in trust. His lender didn't object because of the Garn–St. Germain Act of 1982, which protects transfers into revocable trusts from triggering a "due-on-sale" clause.

Control doesn't disappear

One of the biggest fears people have is: "If I put my house in a trust, do I lose control?" The answer: not if you set it up properly.

- In the UK, if you name yourself trustee, you still control the house. You can live there, maintain it, even sell it (with lender consent).
- In the US, if you use a revocable living trust and name yourself trustee, you still have full control. You can revoke it anytime.

The only time you "lose control" is if you intentionally set up an irrevocable trust or give trustees wide powers without including yourself. For most homeowners, that's unnecessary.

What makes trusts powerful

So why bother? If you still own the house and still pay the mortgage, why add this extra step? Because the trust changes what happens when you die or if you become incapacitated.

- In the **UK**, trusts help protect against probate delays, inheritance disputes, and sometimes inheritance tax planning. They're especially useful for blended families (children from different marriages).
- In the **US**, trusts help property pass outside of probate, avoid court costs, and give clear instructions about who gets what and when.

Think of it as moving your house from the messy traffic of probate court into a private fast lane. Same house, same control, smoother journey.

Breaking down the jargon in plain English

Let's take a few words you'll keep hearing:

- **Revocable**: you can change it whenever you want.
- **Irrevocable**: locked in — hard to change.
- **Life Interest**: someone gets to use it for life, but doesn't own it.
- **Discretionary**: trustee chooses who benefits and when.
- **Bare Trust**: just holding it for someone until they're old enough.
- **Settlor / Grantor**: the person who sets it up.
- **Trustee**: the manager.
- **Beneficiary**: the one who benefits.

That's all you need to know.

Case example comparison

UK example: David in Bristol transferred his semi-detached into a discretionary trust with himself as sole trustee and his children as beneficiaries. His only cost was the Land Registry fee (£305), ID1 verification (£12), and printing. Under £350. His mortgage stayed the same, and Santander's charge remained on the register.

US example: Maria in Texas transferred her ranch-style home into a revocable living trust. She used a quitclaim deed ($35 recording fee) and notarisation ($15). The whole process was under $100. She kept paying her mortgage as normal, and her county title records now list her trust instead of her personally.

Both ended up with the same result: their kids inherit smoothly, without paying lawyers thousands.

The bottom line of what a trust is

Strip away the legal words and a trust is simple:

- You (settlor) decide the rules.
- You (trustee) hold legal title.
- Your kids or family (beneficiaries) benefit later.

It's a legal container for your house. That's all.

Key takeaways

- A trust is not complicated: three roles (settlor, trustee, beneficiaries).
- In the UK, common forms are life interest and discretionary trusts.
- In the US, the revocable living trust is the go-to option for homeowners.
- You don't lose control if you're the trustee of your own trust.
- Trusts keep inheritance smooth, reduce costs, and prevent probate headaches.
- Cost is modest: a few hundred pounds or dollars.

Chapter 2 – Why Put Your House into a Trust?

The question that nags at people

If you've read this far, you already know what a trust is in simple terms. But you might still be wondering: *Why should I bother putting my house into a trust at all?* After all, you're still paying the mortgage. You still live in the same house. Nothing seems to change today.

That's a fair point. On the surface, it looks like paperwork for paperwork's sake. But here's the deal: the power of a trust isn't about today. It's about tomorrow. It's about what happens when life throws the inevitable at you — death, incapacity, family disputes, or just plain bad timing.

So let's slow down and unpack the reasons. Some of them are about **saving money**. Some are about **saving time**. And some are about **saving your family from stress and conflict**.

The probate problem

Probate is the legal process that happens after someone dies. In the UK, it's called "grant of probate." In the US, it's the probate court system. Same idea: the court has to confirm the will, approve who inherits, and transfer property legally.

Sounds straightforward, right? Not really. Probate can drag on for months, even years. According to UK government data, the average probate application now takes **nine months to complete** (UK Ministry of Justice, 2023). In the US, the American Bar

Association reports that probate can take **six to eighteen months**, and longer if family members argue.

Now imagine your children waiting all that time just to take ownership of the house. Maybe they want to sell it. Maybe they want to live in it. Either way, they're stuck until probate is finished. And while probate is happening, bills pile up, taxes don't wait, and family arguments can brew.

A trust bypasses all that. When your house is in a trust, the trustee doesn't need to wait for probate. They already hold the legal title. They can move forward immediately.

Case example:

- In the UK, Peter from Birmingham died leaving his house to his three kids in his will. Probate took 14 months because of backlog at the Probate Registry. His kids paid council tax, insurance, and maintenance on the empty house the whole time.
- Meanwhile, Susan in Bristol had already placed her terraced home into a discretionary trust with her daughter as replacement trustee. When Susan passed, her daughter became trustee instantly. No probate delays. The house was sold within two months, and the money distributed as Susan had planned.

The difference? Thousands saved, months of stress avoided.

The cost problem

Let's talk money. Probate isn't just slow. It's expensive.

- In the **UK**, probate fees are £273 plus solicitor fees if you use one (Law Society, 2022). Many solicitors charge a percentage of the estate value, often **1–2%**. On a £250,000 home, that could be £2,500–£5,000 gone in fees.

- In the **US**, probate costs range from **2–7% of the estate value**, depending on the state (Nolo Legal Encyclopedia, 2023). So for a $300,000 home, that's $6,000–$21,000.

And that's money your kids or spouse lose — money that could have been avoided if the property was already in a trust.

A trust doesn't eliminate every cost (you'll still pay Land Registry fees in the UK or recording fees in the US), but it cuts out the probate middleman. The savings are real.

The family conflict problem

Here's the part people don't always like to talk about. Death brings out emotions, and sometimes it brings out fights. Even the closest families can get tangled in disagreements about inheritance.

Probate makes it worse. Because the process is public, anyone can challenge it. In the UK, the number of contested wills has risen sharply in recent years (The Guardian, 2022). In the US, contested wills are one of the most common family disputes in probate courts.

A trust makes things clearer. The trustee already has authority. The rules are already set. That doesn't mean families never fight, but it reduces the chance of a messy legal battle.

Case example:

- John in Texas left his house by will to his three children. His eldest challenged it in probate, arguing Dad had promised him the house outright. The fight lasted two years, drained $40,000 in legal fees, and destroyed family ties.

- Compare with Rachel in London, who had put her semi into a life interest trust. Her husband could live there for life, and after his death, the house went to her daughters. Clear. No arguments. The trust deed spoke louder than emotions.

The incapacity problem

Death isn't the only issue. What happens if you're alive but can't make decisions? Maybe illness, dementia, or an accident leaves you unable to handle your affairs.

- In the UK, if you lose mental capacity and your house isn't in a trust, someone may need to apply to the **Court of Protection** to manage it. That process is slow and costly.
- In the US, if you become incapacitated, your family may need a **guardianship** or **conservatorship** order to deal with your home. Again, court involvement, again expensive.

A trust avoids this. If you name yourself trustee but also appoint a replacement trustee (like Narberth in our earlier draft), then if something happens to you, your replacement steps in seamlessly. No court, no delay.

The blended family problem

Here's a scenario that comes up all the time: second marriages.

Let's say you own a home. You marry again. You want your new spouse to be secure if you die, but you also want your children from your first marriage to inherit eventually. A will often fails here because it either leaves the house to the spouse (kids cut out) or to the kids (spouse left vulnerable).

A trust solves it neatly:

- You set up a **life interest trust** giving your spouse the right to live in the house for life.
- When they die or move out, the property passes to your children.

Case example: Alan in Bristol remarried at 60. His new wife needed security, but his two grown-up sons were his priority for inheritance. He used a life interest trust for under £400 in fees. His wife had a home for life, and his sons had guaranteed inheritance later. Everyone felt secure.

The lender problem (and why it's not a problem)

A lot of homeowners hesitate because of one worry: *"If I put my mortgaged house in a trust, will my bank call in the loan?"*

In the UK, lenders like Santander or Nationwide do require consent. But if you remain the borrower and trustee, they usually agree. The charge (mortgage) stays on the title. They still get their money.

In the US, the Garn–St. Germain Act of 1982 specifically says that putting a home into a revocable living trust **does not trigger the due-on-sale clause**. That means your lender cannot demand full repayment just because you moved your house into a trust.

So while you do need to notify your lender, it's not the roadblock many think it is.

Control is still in your hands

This fear comes up over and over: "If my house is in a trust, do I still control it?" The short answer: yes, if you set it up right.

- In the UK, name yourself trustee. You keep full control.
- In the US, use a revocable living trust. You keep full control.

You can sell, refinance, or live in the property. The only difference is that when you die or become incapacitated, the trust makes the transition smooth.

The peace of mind factor

Sometimes the real reason is simpler: peace of mind. Knowing your spouse won't face months of paperwork. Knowing your kids won't fight. Knowing the court won't get involved.

Case example: Maria in Leeds admitted she didn't fully grasp all the tax rules, but she said this: *"I sleep better knowing it's sorted. My kids won't have to figure it out."* That's worth more than any lawyer's jargon.

Quick recap of the main reasons

- **Avoid probate delays and costs**
- **Protect against family disputes**

- **Prepare for incapacity**
- **Protect blended families**
- **Keep control while alive**
- **Save thousands in fees**
- **Buy peace of mind**

Key takeaways

- Probate is slow and costly in both the UK and US. A trust avoids it.
- Trusts save thousands by cutting out probate fees and solicitor/attorney costs.
- They reduce family conflict by setting clear rules.
- They protect you if you become incapacitated.
- They're especially powerful in blended families.
- Your lender won't block you if you handle it properly.
- You don't lose control if you're trustee of your own trust.
- The real gain is peace of mind for you and your family.

Chapter 3 – The Costs

Why people think it costs thousands

Ask around and you'll hear horror stories: a solicitor in London quoted £2,500 to set up a life interest trust for a modest terraced house. An attorney in California charged a widow $4,000 for a revocable living trust "estate package." A couple in Manchester told me they walked out of a legal office with a three-page deed and a bill for £1,900. Why so high? Because professionals wrap a fairly simple process in layers of "service."

Part of this is understandable. Lawyers charge for time, not just forms. They cover themselves for every "what if" scenario. They anticipate disputes, taxes, edge cases. The problem is that the average homeowner doesn't need a Rolls Royce when a reliable bicycle will do the job.

Here's the truth: if your goal is to **move your house into a trust for straightforward estate planning** — not for complex tax shelters or corporate structures — you can do it legally for a fraction of what you've been told. The price tag? **Under £400 in the UK. Under $600 in the US.**

Now let's break it down, step by step, so you can see where the money goes, where people waste it, and how to keep your total under that line.

The UK cost breakdown

Let's start with the UK because the Land Registry process is a bit stricter. Here's where your money actually goes:

1. **Land Registry Fee**

- o This is the unavoidable core cost.
- o Fees depend on property value:
    - Up to £80,000 → £45
    - £80,001–£100,000 → £95
    - £100,001–£200,000 → £230
    - Over £200,000 → £305
- o Example: A typical home in Bristol worth £260,000 will cost **£305** to register into a trust.

2. **Identity Verification (Form ID1)**
   - o Required if you're not using a solicitor.
   - o Cost at HM Land Registry office: £12.
   - o Cost at solicitor/conveyancer: £40–£60 per person.
   - o If you're sole trustee, you only need one verification: **£12–£60**.

3. **Trust Deed**
   - o DIY using a clear template: **£0**.
   - o If you ask a solicitor to draft it: **£500–£1,500**.
   - o Example: Theo in Bristol used a simple discretionary trust deed he drafted himself for £0.

4. **Postage and Copies**
   - o Special Delivery to Land Registry: ~£8.
   - o Certified copies of the deed (optional but smart): ~£20.

UK Total (DIY route): ~£350 (for a house over £200,000).
UK Total (with solicitor drafting deed): £1,000–£2,000+.

The US cost breakdown

In the US, the process is different but the same principle applies: the only unavoidable costs are the county recorder's fee and notarisation.

1. **County Recorder Fee**

- o Varies widely by county.
- o Some charge a flat fee ($50–$100).
- o Others charge per page ($15–$30 per page, often 3–5 pages).
- o Example: In Harris County, Texas, the fee is $26 for the first page and $4 for each additional page. A 4-page quitclaim deed costs $38.

2. **Notarisation**
   - o Required for deeds.
   - o Average fee: $10–$20 per signature.
   - o Some states cap notary fees (e.g., California $15 per signature).
   - o Mobile notaries cost more but aren't necessary if you plan ahead.

3. **Trust Agreement**
   - o DIY with a revocable living trust template: **$0–$50**.
   - o Attorney-drafted trust agreement: **$1,000–$3,000**.
   - o Example: James in Ohio bought a $40 template, filled it in with his wife, and notarised it. Done.

4. **Other Small Costs**
   - o Copies of recorded deed: $5–$15.
   - o Binder or digital storage for trust documents: $10–$20.

US Total (DIY route): $100–$300.
US Total (with attorney drafting trust): $2,000–$5,000+.

Where people waste money

1. **Paying for things they don't need**
   - o Most homeowners only need a **basic discretionary trust (UK)** or **revocable living trust (US)**. Paying for complex "asset protection"

structures is overkill unless you're shielding millions.

2. **Solicitor/attorney drafting**
   - o Legal professionals add cost. Yes, they provide tailored advice, but if your situation is straightforward, you're paying thousands for what can be done for hundreds.
3. **Multiple trustees requiring ID checks**
   - o Some people name all their children as trustees from the start. That means ID1 fees for everyone in the UK, or multiple notarisation fees in the US. It's cheaper to start as sole trustee and name replacements in the deed.
4. **Unnecessary copies**
   - o Paying £100 for "official bound copies" of your trust deed is pointless when you can print and certify for £20.

Case example: UK

Theo (fictional composite) owns a semi-detached in Bristol worth £260,000 with a Santander mortgage. His solicitor quoted £1,800 to set up a discretionary trust. Theo used a DIY trust deed template, filled in TR1 and AP1, got ID1 verified at Land Registry for £12, and sent the pack with £305 fee. His total outlay: **£322**. Santander confirmed the charge stayed in place.

Case example: US

Maria in California wanted her home in a revocable living trust so her kids would avoid probate. Her attorney quoted $3,500. Maria downloaded a template for $50, notarised it for $15, filled

in a quitclaim deed, and recorded it at the county office for $95.
Her total outlay: **$160**.

How to keep it under £400 or $600

- **UK:**
    - DIY trust deed (free template).
    - Sole trustee (one ID1 check only).
    - Land Registry fee (£305 for most houses).
    - Postage and copies (~£20).
    - Total: ~£340.
- **US:**
    - Revocable living trust template ($50).
    - Notary ($20).
    - County recorder fee ($50–$150).
    - Copies and storage (~$20).
    - Total: ~ $200.

What about hidden taxes?

- **UK:** Stamp Duty Land Tax (SDLT) only applies if money changes hands or the trust assumes mortgage debt. If you remain personally liable for the mortgage, **no SDLT.**
- **US:** No federal tax for putting your personal home into a revocable living trust. It's not a sale. Some states have transfer taxes, but they usually exempt transfers into trusts.

The fear vs. the facts

- **Fear:** "It costs thousands to set up a trust."
- **Fact:** Under £400 or $600 if done correctly.
- **Fear:** "The bank will force me to refinance."
- **Fact:** Lender consent in UK, Garn–St. Germain Act in US protects you.
- **Fear:** "I'll lose control of my house."
- **Fact:** If you're trustee, you remain in control.

Key takeaways

- The real unavoidable costs are modest: Land Registry (£305 UK) or county recording + notary ($100–$200 US).
- Identity verification is cheap if you're sole trustee.
- DIY trust deeds save hundreds or thousands.
- Avoid solicitor/attorney packages unless your case is truly complex.
- The realistic DIY total: **£350 UK, $200–$300 US**.
- Always confirm taxes, but for most homeowners, no extra duty applies.

Chapter 4 – The Step-by-Step Process (UK)

Starting where it matters most

If you live in the UK and you're ready to put your home into a trust, this is the chapter you'll dog-ear, highlight, and probably come back to at 2 AM when you can't sleep. Why? Because this is the part that turns theory into action. No more abstract talk about probate or inheritance — here's the hands-on "how."

You'll see how to do it in the simplest possible way, with clear forms, a realistic budget, and none of the confusing filler that makes most guides unreadable. The goal: get your house safely into a trust without wasting more than **£400**.

Step 1. Check your mortgage agreement

Let's be honest. If you have a mortgage, your lender has a say. Flip through your paperwork and you'll almost certainly find a "due-on-sale" or "alienation" clause. This is lawyer-speak for: "If you transfer the house to someone else, we can demand repayment of the loan."

Sounds scary, right? But in practice, most lenders in the UK don't call in loans when you transfer property into a trust — as long as:

- You remain personally liable for the mortgage.
- The lender's charge (their security over your house) stays on the Land Registry title.

Banks just want their money. They don't care who technically holds the title as long as their charge is safe.

Case in point: A couple in Manchester called Nationwide when planning to put their house into a discretionary trust. The lender's reply was simple: "As long as our charge remains and you keep paying, we're fine." Always ask for this in writing.

Step 2. Ask your lender for consent

Here's where you need a short, clear letter. Keep it professional, not emotional. You're not asking permission to stop paying — you're simply confirming you want to transfer legal title into a trust while still carrying the mortgage.

What to include in your letter:

- Your name and mortgage account number.
- The property address.
- Statement that you'll remain personally liable.
- Statement that the mortgage charge will stay on the title.
- Type of trust (life interest, discretionary).
- Date you want to complete.

Expect a reply within a few weeks. File the consent letter with your trust paperwork — HM Land Registry may ask for it.

Step 3. Draft your trust deed

This is the beating heart of the process. The trust deed sets out:

- Who the settlor is (you).
- Who the trustee(s) are (you, or you plus others).

- Who the beneficiaries are (your kids, spouse, family).
- Replacement trustees (e.g., Narberth becomes trustee if Theo dies).
- The rules about selling, living in, or benefiting from the property.

A discretionary trust is the most flexible. A life interest trust is best if you want a spouse to live in the house until death but eventually pass it to children.

You don't need fancy parchment. A signed, witnessed deed on plain A4 with the right clauses works perfectly. Just make sure each trustee signs and each signature has an independent adult witness.

Step 4. Fill in TR1 transfer form

The TR1 is the Land Registry's way of saying: "Who owns this property now?" It's the official transfer of title.

- **Box 1:** Date of transfer (e.g., 21 August 2025).
- **Box 2:** Title number (from your title register).
- **Box 3:** Property address.
- **Box 4:** Transferor = your name and address.
- **Box 5:** Transferee = "Tom Jerry of 123 London Road, London, Postcode as Trustee of The Tom Jerry's Family Discretionary Trust."
- **Box 6:** Consideration = "No monetary consideration. Transfer into trust subject to existing Santander Bank charge."
- **Box 9:** Title guarantee = "Full title guarantee."
- **Box 11:** Declaration of trust = "The property is transferred to the trustee to hold on the terms of The Tom Jerry's Family Discretionary Trust Deed dated 21 August 2025."

- **Execution section:** Sign in front of a witness.

That's the TR1 done. It looks scarier than it is.

Step 5. Fill in AP1 application form

The AP1 tells Land Registry: "Update the register with this transfer."

Key parts:

- Title number.
- Applicant: your name as trustee.
- Property address.
- Type of application: "Transfer of whole registered title into trust."
- Documents lodged: TR1, trust deed, lender consent letter, ID1, cheque for fee.
- Existing charges: list Santander Bank plc.
- Consideration: "None (gift into trust)."
- Signature: sign and date.

Step 6. Verify your identity (Form ID1)

Because you're not using a solicitor, Land Registry wants to confirm it's really you. This means filling out Form ID1 and getting it verified.

What you'll need:

- Passport or photocard driving licence.
- 1 passport-style photo.
- Completed ID1 form.

Where to get it verified:

- HM Land Registry office: £12.
- Solicitor or conveyancer: £40–£60.

Only you need this, since you're the only trustee. Beneficiaries don't count.

Step 7. Pay the Land Registry fee

This depends on your property's value:

- Over £200,000: £305 (most UK homes).
- Under £200,000: £230.
- Lower bands: £45–£95.

Make your cheque payable to "HM Land Registry."

Step 8. Submit your pack

Put it all together:

1. Cover letter (simple explanation).
2. AP1 form.
3. TR1 form.
4. Signed trust deed.
5. Santander consent letter.
6. ID1 form.
7. Cheque for fee.

Post to:
HM Land Registry
Citizen Centre

PO Box 74
Gloucester
GL14 9BB

Clip, don't staple. They scan everything.

Step 9. Wait for the updated title

Processing can take a few weeks. Once done, your title register will say something like:

"Proprietor: Tom Jerry'of 123 London Road, London, Postcode, as Trustee of The Tom Jerry's Family Discretionary Trust."

The Santander charge will remain listed. You keep paying your mortgage as normal.

Step 10. Update insurance

Call your home insurer. Tell them:

- You're still policyholder.
- The trust is an additional interested party.

They'll note it. No big change in premium.

Checkpoint: how much did this cost?

- Trust deed (DIY): £0.
- TR1, AP1, ID1 forms: free to download.
- ID verification: £12.

- Land Registry fee (house > £200k): £305.
- Postage/copies: £20.

Total: £337.

That's it. Not £1,800. Not £2,500. Under £400, start to finish.

Case study: Theo's Bristol home

Idris Douglas Mather owns 1000 James Road, Brighton, worth £260,000, with a Barclays mortgage. He:

- Wrote to Santander, got consent.
- Drafted a discretionary trust deed with himself as trustee and his children as beneficiaries.
- Completed TR1 (transfer to trust) and AP1 (application to update).
- Did ID1 at Land Registry for £12.
- Paid £305 fee.

Within 5 weeks, Land Registry updated the title. Santander's charge stayed. Idris Douglas Mather's kids now have peace of mind: when he dies, the property passes smoothly, no probate delays.

Key takeaways

- The UK process looks complex but boils down to three forms (TR1, AP1, ID1), a trust deed, and a fee.
- Lender consent is required, but most banks allow it.
- If you're sole trustee, only you need ID verification.
- Total cost is under £400 for most UK homes.

33

- Your mortgage continues as normal — nothing changes day to day.
- The payoff is avoiding probate, saving thousands, and protecting your family.

Chapter 5 – The Step-by-Step Process (US)

The American reality check

If you've heard of living trusts in the United States, chances are you've also heard scary price tags. Attorneys quote **$2,000–$5,000 packages**, bundled with "estate planning services" and a lot of leather-bound folders that look impressive but don't actually change the mechanics of what happens to your house.

Here's the truth: you can legally set up a **revocable living trust**, move your home into it, and protect your family from probate — all without paying more than **$400–$600 total**. That's not a loophole. It's simply the law. And if you can fill out basic forms, you can do this yourself.

Let's break the process down into real steps, with plain explanations and examples from families across the U.S.

Step 1. Decide on the type of trust

In the U.S., the gold standard for homeowners is the **revocable living trust**.

- *Revocable* means you can change it, revoke it, or update beneficiaries while you're alive.
- *Living* means it takes effect now, not just when you die.
- *Trust* means legal ownership shifts into the trust, but you still control everything as trustee.

Alternative trusts exist (irrevocable, special needs, charitable), but unless you're ultra-wealthy or need advanced tax sheltering, a standard revocable living trust is enough.

Example: Maria in California wanted her two kids to inherit her San Diego condo without the state's notorious 18-month probate delay. A revocable living trust let her stay in full control while guaranteeing her kids wouldn't be stuck in court.

Step 2. Draft your trust document

This is the central contract, like the UK's trust deed. It spells out:

- Who the **grantor/settlor** is (you, the homeowner).
- Who the **trustee(s)** are (you, while alive).
- Who the **successor trustee(s)** are (your replacement upon death or incapacity).
- Who the **beneficiaries** are (kids, spouse, relatives, or even charities).
- The rules: who lives there, how it can be sold, how proceeds are divided.

You can:

- Write it yourself using state-specific templates (often $50–$100 online).
- Buy a DIY trust kit.
- Use an online platform like LegalZoom ($200–$400).

The trust must be signed, notarized, and ideally witnessed (varies by state).

Step 3. Prepare a new deed

Here's where many people trip up. To move your property into the trust, you need a new **deed** transferring ownership from yourself (person) to yourself (as trustee of the trust).

The type of deed depends on your state:

- **Quitclaim Deed** – simple, often used between family or into trust.
- **Warranty Deed** – stronger guarantees, used in some states.
- **Grant Deed** – common in California and Western states.

The wording usually looks like this:

"I, John Smith, hereby transfer and quitclaim to John Smith, Trustee of The Smith Family Revocable Living Trust dated September 1, 2025, the following property…"

Then you include the legal description from your existing deed (not just the street address).

Case example: In Texas, James and Elaine moved their family ranch into a revocable living trust using a warranty deed. Their county clerk insisted on precise metes-and-bounds wording from their old deed. They simply copied it word for word. Done.

Step 4. Get the deed notarized

Unlike the UK, where you just need a witness, the U.S. system demands a **notary public**. This adds weight and stops fraud.

Cost: usually **$10–$25** per document at banks, UPS stores, or your county clerk's office. Some states let you use online notaries.

Bring:

- Government ID.
- Printed deed.
- Yourself (the grantor) in person.

You sign in front of the notary, they stamp it, and now it's legally valid.

Step 5. Record the deed at the county recorder's office

This is the step that makes it "official" in public records. Every county has a **recorder (sometimes called Register of Deeds, or Clerk & Recorder)**.

Process:

- Take the signed trust deed and new transfer deed.
- Pay a small recording fee (usually **$25–$75**).
- Clerk scans, stamps, and files it.
- You get a certified copy for your records.

Timeline: same day in many counties, or a few weeks for mailed filings.

Now the public record shows: John Smith, Trustee of The Smith Family Revocable Living Trust, owns the property.

Step 6. Update insurance and mortgage lender

Your homeowner's insurance should reflect that the house is held in trust. Call your insurer, give them the trust name, and they'll note it as an "additional insured." Premium usually doesn't change.

As for the mortgage lender: just like in the UK, federal law (the Garn-St. Germain Act of 1982) stops banks from calling in your loan when you transfer your home into a revocable living trust. The key is:

- You stay borrower.
- You stay resident.
- Lender's lien remains untouched.

So you don't need permission, but some banks like a courtesy letter.

Step 7. Store your documents safely

At this point, you'll have:

- Revocable living trust (notarized).
- Original deed transferring property to trust.
- Certified copy of recorded deed.
- Insurance update confirmation.

Keep copies in a fireproof safe and give one to your successor trustee. If you only stash it in a shoebox under the bed, you're asking for chaos later.

Step 8. Consider other assets

While your house is the big one, you can also add:

- Bank accounts.
- Investment accounts.
- Vehicles.
- Life insurance policies.

Each transfer has its own paperwork. For now, securing your home is the major milestone.

Step 9. Check state-specific quirks

Different states = different rules.

- **California**: Requires a "Preliminary Change of Ownership Report" when recording a deed. Failing to file can trigger reassessment.
- **Florida**: Homestead rules mean you must be careful not to accidentally disinherit a spouse.
- **Texas**: Property description must be exact (metes and bounds).
- **New York**: Transfer tax may apply if not done correctly.

Always check your county website for "trust deed recording requirements." They usually publish checklists.

Step 10. Cost breakdown (U.S.)

Let's add it up.

- Trust drafting (DIY kit or online): $50–$400.
- New deed preparation: $0 (if you copy old one) or $50 (online template).
- Notary: $10–$25.
- County recording fee: $25–$75.

- Copies/postage: $20.

Total: $105–$570.

That's it. Not thousands. And once it's done, your home is fully trust-protected.

Case Study: The Johnsons in Ohio

- Home: $280,000 in Columbus.
- Mortgage: still paying Chase Bank.
- Steps:
    - Drafted revocable living trust using a $90 online service.
    - Prepared quitclaim deed from themselves to themselves as trustees.
    - Signed and notarized at UPS Store for $10.
    - Recorded deed with Franklin County Recorder for $34.
- Total cost: $134.

Result: Their kids won't face Ohio probate, which often takes 12–18 months. The property will transfer seamlessly.

Checkpoint: Are you really done?

If you've:

- Signed a trust.
- Transferred title with a deed.
- Recorded it at county.
- Updated insurance.

Then yes — your home is officially in your trust. Probate avoided. Mission accomplished.

Key takeaways

- In the U.S., the central tool is the **revocable living trust**.
- You don't need a lawyer — DIY kits and online platforms work fine.
- Recording the deed makes it official.
- Federal law protects you from banks demanding repayment when you transfer into trust.
- Total cost is under $600 in nearly all states.
- State quirks exist — check county requirements to avoid mistakes.

Chapter 6 – Mistakes and How to Avoid Them

Why this matters

So, you've decided to put your property into a trust. Great. But here's the catch: a lot of people mess it up. Not because they're careless, but because the process feels foreign. One wrong move doesn't usually mean disaster — but it can mean delays, extra costs, or even making the trust useless.

The good news? Every mistake I'm about to cover is **100% avoidable**. Once you see them spelled out, you'll notice how easy it is to stay on track.

Mistake 1. Forgetting to actually register the transfer

This one's surprisingly common. People sign a shiny new trust deed, pat themselves on the back, and then stop. But here's the thing: a trust deed alone doesn't move the legal ownership. It sets the rules, yes, but unless you file the proper transfer (TR1 in the UK, deed of transfer in the US), Land Registry or the County Recorder's Office still shows you as the individual owner.

The result? Probate still applies. The property is not officially in the trust. Your family ends up right back in court.

Case example (UK): Fiona in Birmingham created a family trust in 2018 but never filed the TR1. When she passed in 2022, her sons were shocked to find the house still in her sole name. The trust meant nothing without the registered transfer. They had to go through probate anyway, costing them £6,000 in legal fees.

How to avoid: Always follow the paperwork through. Trust deed + TR1 + AP1 (UK). Trust deed + deed of trust transfer recorded with county (US). Until the registry or recorder updates the title, it's not done.

Mistake 2. Leaving out successor trustees

If you're the only trustee and you die or become incapacitated, who's left to manage the trust? If you didn't name anyone, the court decides. That means your "DIY to save money" project suddenly becomes a court matter.

Case example (US): In Illinois, Mark set up a living trust but only named himself as trustee. When he passed away unexpectedly, his kids had to petition the court to appoint a replacement trustee. That delayed access to the house for nearly a year.

How to avoid: Always, always name at least one successor trustee in your trust deed. It can be a family member, close friend, or even a professional (though professionals often charge). This one step removes a ton of risk.

Mistake 3. Not telling your mortgage lender

A lot of homeowners are terrified their bank will call the loan due if they move the house into a trust. That's extremely rare. Banks generally don't mind, because you're still the borrower and their mortgage still attaches to the property.

The problem arises when you fail to tell them. Later, if you refinance or sell, the bank spots the trust transfer and delays the process until they get confirmation.

Case example (UK): James in Manchester transferred his property into trust but didn't notify Halifax. A year later, he wanted to remortgage. Halifax nearly refused until he produced the trust documents and signed a consent form. It added 6 stressful weeks.

How to avoid: Always send your lender a copy of the trust deed and transfer notice. In the UK, most banks just file it. In the US, many will want a one-page consent letter.

Mistake 4. Forgetting your insurance company

Here's a sneaky one. You put your house into a trust but keep the insurance in your personal name. A fire breaks out. You file a claim. The insurer spots the trust name on the property title and says, "Sorry, the insured party doesn't match the legal owner." Claim denied.

Case example (US): A California homeowner transferred her property into a revocable trust but didn't tell her insurer. When a storm destroyed the roof, the insurer initially denied the claim. She had to fight for months before it was sorted out.

How to avoid: Call your insurer as soon as the trust is recorded. Ask them to update the policy to list the trustee of the trust as an insured party. Takes 5 minutes. Could save hundreds of thousands.

Mistake 5. Naming minor children directly as beneficiaries

Parents often think: "I'll just leave the house to my kids." But if your kids are under 18 (UK) or under 21 in some US states, they legally can't manage property. That means the court appoints someone. Suddenly, you've got a court-appointed stranger handling your child's inheritance.

Case example (UK): Lucy left her London home to her 15-year-old son through a simple trust deed. When she died, the court had to appoint a professional trustee until he turned 18. That trustee charged £2,500 in fees over 3 years.

How to avoid: Use the trust itself to set conditions. Instead of naming minors directly, the trust says: "Property to be held for the benefit of my children until age 25." That way, the trustee (you, and later your successor) manages things responsibly.

Mistake 6. Not keeping copies in a safe place

This sounds obvious, but trust deeds and transfer documents do get lost. Without them, proving the trust exists can be a nightmare.

Case example (US): In Texas, a family misplaced their original trust deed. Years later, when selling the home, the buyer's lawyer refused to close until a certified copy was found. It took 3 months of digging through county archives.

How to avoid: Keep copies in three places:

- Fireproof safe at home.
- With your successor trustee.
- Digital scan stored securely (USB drive or cloud).

Mistake 7. Not updating after major life changes

Life changes fast. Divorce, new children, new partners, moving house. If your trust doesn't reflect reality, your beneficiaries might get cut out — or the wrong people benefit.

Case example (UK): Alan set up a trust leaving his house to his wife and two sons. Ten years later, he divorced and remarried but never updated the trust. When he died, his ex-wife still had rights as a beneficiary. Ugly court battle followed.

How to avoid: Review your trust every 3–5 years, or after big life events. Updating is easy — either amend the deed or create a new one.

Mistake 8. Believing a trust avoids all taxes

This one trips up a lot of people. In the UK, trusts don't magically eliminate inheritance tax (IHT). In the US, trusts don't avoid federal estate tax if your estate is over the exemption limit.

Case example: Emma in Kent thought her discretionary trust meant no IHT. Wrong — HMRC still counted the property value above the nil-rate band. Her children had to pay £40,000.

How to avoid: A trust is about control and avoiding probate, not dodging tax. Always check tax implications separately with HMRC (UK) or IRS rules (US).

Mistake 9. DIY without double-checking the forms

DIY is fine. In fact, I encourage it. But skipping details — like the title number on a TR1, or the exact legal property description — can mean your application gets rejected.

Case example (UK): A homeowner in Sheffield left the postcode off the AP1. Land Registry sent everything back. Another 4 weeks lost.

How to avoid: Double-check every form before sending. Have a friend look over it if needed.

Mistake 10. Not funding the trust properly

In the US especially, creating a living trust is step one. But you also need to "fund" it by transferring your property, bank accounts, and other assets. If you forget, the trust is an empty shell.

Case example (US): A couple in Florida paid $1,200 to have a trust drafted but never transferred their house into it. When they died, probate court still took over. The trust sat unused.

How to avoid: After signing the deed, record it with the county and re-title the property. Without this, the trust does nothing.

Checkpoint moment

Still with me? Notice the pattern: most mistakes aren't about complicated law. They're about follow-through. People stop too early, forget to tell someone, or fail to keep things updated.

Key takeaways

- Trust deeds alone aren't enough. Always register the transfer.

- Name at least one successor trustee to avoid court intervention.
- Notify both lender and insurer — two quick calls that prevent chaos.
- Don't name minors directly. Use the trust to set an age of inheritance.
- Keep documents safe and update regularly.
- Trusts don't erase taxes. They erase probate headaches.
- Double-check forms before sending.

Top 10 Quick Fix Checklist

(Print this page. Stick it on your fridge. Hand a copy to your trustee. This keeps the whole process simple and safe.)

Mistake People Make	The Quick Fix Solution
1. Signing a trust deed but not registering the transfer	Always file TR1 + AP1 in the UK, or record the deed with your County Recorder in the US
2. Forgetting to name successor trustees	Always list at least one replacement trustee in the deed
3. Not telling the mortgage lender	Send lender a copy of the trust deed and get their written consent (usually routine)
4. Not telling the insurance company	Call your insurer and add "Trustee of [Your Name] Trust" as an insured party
5. Naming under-18s/21s directly as beneficiaries	Use trust language that holds property until children reach a chosen age
6. Losing documents	Keep three copies: home safe, successor trustee, digital scan
7. Ignoring life changes	Review and update your trust after divorce, new children, marriage, or buying/selling property
8. Thinking trusts erase all taxes	Accept that trusts avoid probate, not taxes — check HMRC or IRS rules separately
9. Rushing the forms	Double-check every line on TR1/AP1 (UK) or deed forms (US) before sending
10. Forgetting to "fund" the trust	Make sure the property title is re-registered into the trust name (otherwise the trust is empty)

Chapter 7 – How to Save Thousands Without a Lawyer

Why this chapter matters

Let's be honest: the moment you hear the words "legal paperwork" or "property transfer," your first instinct is to assume you need a solicitor (UK) or attorney (US). And sure, plenty of people do hire one. They sit back, pay the bill, and feel safe. But here's the thing: most of the actual work is form-filling, registering documents, and double-checking details. It's not magic.

Lawyers charge high fees not because every step is complicated, but because they package the entire process as something only they can do. The reality? Ordinary homeowners like you can handle most, if not all, of the process themselves — legally, safely, and for a fraction of the cost.

This chapter shows you how.

The cost difference: UK and US at a glance

Before we get into the "how," let's talk numbers.

- **UK (solicitor route):** Expect to pay £1,200–£2,500 in solicitor fees to create and register a trust deed, handle Land Registry paperwork, and liaise with your lender. If inheritance planning is included, it can push closer to £3,000.

- **UK (DIY route):** Around £400–£500 all in:
  - Trust deed template or drafting help: £50–£150
  - Land Registry TR1 and AP1 filing: £40–£60 in fees
  - ID verification and certification of copies: £20–£50
  - Courier/printing: £20–£30
  - Miscellaneous (copies, storage, notary if needed): £50
  - Total: **well under £600**
- **US (attorney route):** Typically $2,000–$5,000 for a full revocable living trust package. Some firms even quote $10,000 if estate tax planning is included.
- **US (DIY route):** Around $400–$600:
  - Trust kit or drafting software: $50–$150
  - County recording fees: $50–$150 depending on state
  - Notarisation fees: $10–$25 per document
  - Copies, storage: $20–$30
  - Optional review (if you pay a paralegal or online legal service to glance over it): $100–$200
  - Total: **under $600**

That's the savings. Thousands left in your pocket — money that could stay with your family rather than going to fees.

Why people overpay

Three myths keep people from trying the DIY path:

1. *"It's illegal to do it yourself."*
   Wrong. Trust law in both the UK and US is built on the principle that private individuals can create and manage trusts. Lawyers help, but they're not required.

2. *"The forms are too complicated."*
   Not really. Government offices (HM Land Registry in the UK, County Recorders in the US) design forms for the general public. If you can fill in a mortgage application or passport renewal, you can handle this.
3. *"I'll get sued if I get it wrong."*
   What actually happens if you make a mistake? Usually, the registry or recorder rejects the form, tells you what's missing, and gives you another chance. It's more like applying for a driver's licence than going to court.

Breaking down the process: UK

Let's walk through the UK version of doing this without a solicitor.

Step 1. Draft the trust deed

- Cost: £50–£150 if you use a template service or hire a paralegal to draft.
- What it is: A legal document naming you (the settlor and trustee), listing beneficiaries, setting the rules, and naming successor trustees.
- DIY tip: Keep it simple. State who holds the property, who benefits, and how decisions are made.

Step 2. Fill out the TR1 (transfer form)

- This moves the property from your personal name into the trust.
- You'll need your property's title number (find it on your title register).
- TR1 includes: transferor (you), transferee (you as trustee of the trust), and the property details.
- Cost: Free to download. Filing fee is £40–£60.

Step 3. Complete the AP1 (application form)

- This notifies HM Land Registry to update the title.
- It links the trust deed and TR1.
- DIY tip: Attach certified copies of the trust deed.

Step 4. Verify your ID (Form ID1)

- If you don't use a solicitor, you need to prove your identity directly to Land Registry.
- Cost: Usually £20–£50 with a notary or regulated professional.
- You only need this once, unless you transfer again.

Step 5. Notify your lender and insurer

- Send Santander, Barclays, or whoever your lender is a copy of the trust deed and transfer.
- Call your insurance company and ask them to update the "named insured."
- Cost: Free.

Step 6. Store your documents safely

- Fireproof safe, digital scan, and give a copy to your successor trustee.

Total cost: Around £400–£500.

Breaking down the process: US

The US version is similar but with state-level variations. Here's the general flow:

Step 1. Draft the living trust agreement

- Cost: $50–$150 using a legal template or online kit.
- What it includes: Name of the trust, trustee (you), beneficiaries, successor trustee, rules of distribution.
- DIY tip: Keep clear language. Don't overcomplicate.

Step 2. Prepare a new deed

- Called a "quitclaim deed" or "trust transfer deed" depending on state.
- This transfers the house title from you individually to you as trustee of the trust.
- You'll need the legal property description (from your current deed).

Step 3. Notarise the deed

- Required in all states.
- Cost: $10–$25.
- DIY tip: Banks often notarise for free for account holders.

Step 4. Record the deed with the County Recorder

- This is the big step. You submit the notarised deed, plus the trust agreement if required, and pay the recording fee ($50–$150).
- DIY tip: Many counties let you mail it in or drop it at a service counter.

Step 5. Notify lender and insurer

- Send the bank a copy of the trust.
- Call your insurance company and ask them to add the trust.

Step 6. Store everything properly

- Same as the UK: fireproof safe, scan, backup copy with trustee.

Total cost: Around \$400–\$600.

Case examples of DIY success

UK example:
Sandra in Leeds transferred her £280,000 terraced house into a family trust for under £500. She used free Land Registry forms, bought a £95 trust deed template online, paid £40 in registry fees, and £25 for ID verification. She avoided the £1,800 solicitor quote she was given.

US example:
Joseph and Maria in Ohio created a living trust for their \$220,000 home using a \$129 kit, a \$20 notary, and a \$60 county recording fee. Their attorney had quoted \$3,000. They saved over \$2,700 and got it done in a week.

What you actually need to spend money on

People often ask: "What's the bare minimum I can get away with?" Here's the honest list:

- **UK:** Trust deed drafting (template or professional help for clarity), Land Registry fees, ID verification.
- **US:** Trust agreement, notarisation, county recording fees.

Everything else — courier costs, copies, fireproof safe — is optional but smart.

When DIY may not be enough

Here's me being straight with you. DIY isn't for everyone.
There are a few situations where paying for help is smart:

- Very high-value estates (above £1 million in the UK, or above the federal estate tax threshold in the US).
- Complicated family setups (blended families, estranged relatives, contested wills).
- If you own multiple properties across different countries.
- If you want tax avoidance schemes (beyond simple probate avoidance).

In those cases, a lawyer can add value. But for 80% of ordinary homeowners — one house, spouse, kids — DIY works fine.

How to make it painless

- **Use templates.** Don't try to draft a trust deed from scratch. Kits exist for a reason.
- **Take your time.** Block out one Saturday to do the paperwork.
- **Call the office.** Land Registry staff (UK) and County Recorders (US) are surprisingly helpful. They can't give legal advice, but they can tell you if a form is filled in correctly.
- **Ask a friend to review.** A second pair of eyes catches mistakes.

The psychology of saving money

Here's something interesting: people often feel safer paying thousands because they assume higher cost means higher security. But when you do it yourself, you actually gain a deeper understanding of how the trust works. That makes you more prepared to manage it long-term.

And the savings are real. Imagine using that £2,000/$3,000 you saved:

- Pay down extra on the mortgage.
- Build a holiday fund.
- Add to your child's education savings.
- Cover your own emergency fund.

Why give it away to someone for paperwork you can handle in an afternoon?

Quick side note: scams to avoid

Not all DIY services are trustworthy. Watch out for:

- Companies charging £500/$800 for a "free" Land Registry or county form you could download yourself.
- Aggressive upselling ("You must buy our £2,000 gold package to make your trust valid." Not true).
- Websites that don't clearly say who drafted their templates. Stick to established providers or government websites.

Checkpoint moment

Still with me? Let's recap the key flow.

- Draft the trust agreement/deed.
- Transfer the property title.

- File/register it officially.
- Notify lender and insurer.
- Keep everything safe.

That's it. No solicitor or attorney needed.

Key takeaways

- Lawyers aren't required for most property trust setups — the process is designed for ordinary homeowners.
- DIY costs: £400–£500 in the UK, $400–$600 in the US. Lawyer costs: £1,500–£3,000 in the UK, $2,000–$5,000 in the US.
- The steps are form-based and mostly administrative.
- DIY empowers you to understand your trust better.
- Exceptions exist — complicated estates may still benefit from professional advice.

Cost Comparison: UK vs US (Lawyer vs DIY)

Category	UK – With Solicitor	UK – DIY	US – With Attorney	US – DIY
Trust document drafting	£800–£1,200	£50–£150	$1,500–$2,500	$50–$150
Property transfer deed & filing	£200–£400	£40–£60	$300–$700	$50–$150
ID verification / Notarisation	£50–£100	£20–£50	$100–$200	$10–$25
Registry/County fees	Included in solicitor fee	£40–£60	Included in attorney fee	$50–$150
Document storage/extras	£100–£200	£20–£30	$100–$200	$20–$30

Category	UK – With Solicitor	UK – DIY	US – With Attorney	US – DIY
Total estimated cost	£1,200–£2,500+	£400–£500	$2,000–$5,000+	$400–$600

What this table really shows you

- Paying a professional can be **3 to 5 times more expensive** than doing it yourself.
- Most of that extra money goes to administration, not complex legal work.
- DIY gives you almost the same result — as long as you follow the steps and file correctly.
- Your **savings are real**: about **£1,500–£2,000 in the UK and $2,500–$4,000 in the US**.

DIY vs Lawyer:
Who Should Choose What?

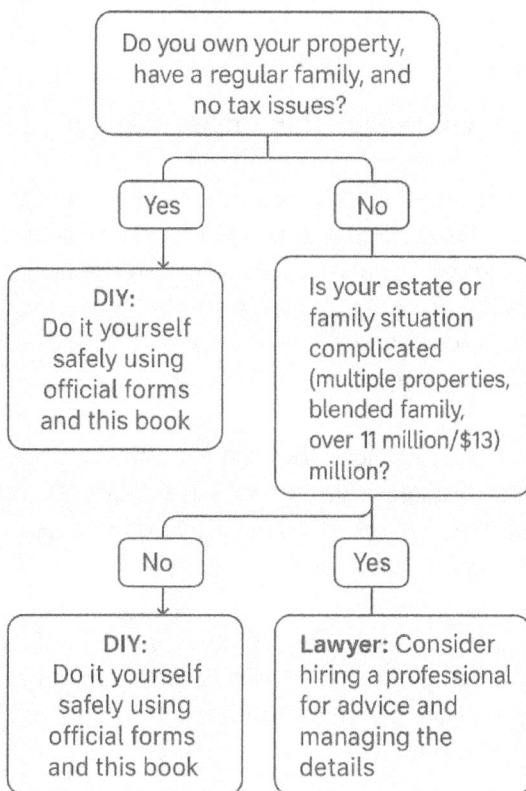

Do you own your property, have a regular family, and no tax issues?

Yes

No

DIY: Do it yourself safely using official forms and this book

Is your estate or family situation complicated (multiple properties, blended family, over 11 million/$13) million?

No

Yes

DIY: Do it yourself safely using official forms and this book

Lawyer: Consider hiring a professional for advice and managing the details

Chapter 8 – Real-Life Stories of Families Who Did It Right

UK Story 1 – The Single Mum in Manchester

Claire was forty-one, a widowed mum of two energetic boys. Her house in Manchester was her pride — a red-brick semi that had seen birthdays, scraped knees, and endless football practice. But after her husband's sudden passing, Claire carried a nagging fear: *what if something happened to me? Who would look after the house for my kids?*

She asked a solicitor once. "For a life interest trust, you're looking at about £2,400, plus VAT," the man said, straight-faced. Claire nearly choked. "That's more than my boys' school trip to France and Christmas combined!"

Instead of walking away defeated, she decided to learn on her own. She spent nights after the boys went to bed researching TR1 forms, trust deeds, and Land Registry rules. Slowly, it made sense. She realised:

- She could be her own trustee.
- She could name her children as beneficiaries.
- She only had to pay **£40 for the Land Registry fee** and about **£20 for ID verification**.

Her moment of panic came when she rang her mortgage lender. "Are you going to penalise me if I put the property in trust?" she asked. The woman on the phone replied calmly, "As long as you remain the trustee, we have no issue. Just send us a copy of the deed." Claire exhaled so loudly her son asked if she was okay.

Total out-of-pocket cost: **£380**. Savings compared to a solicitor: over **£2,000**. More importantly, she knew her sons would not be stuck in probate if the worst happened. "I thought this would be impossible," she told a friend later. "Turns out it was just paperwork and persistence."

UK Story 2 – The Retired Couple in Kent

Alan and Margaret, both in their seventies, lived in a cosy Kent bungalow. They owned it outright after thirty-five years of hard work. One autumn morning, Alan looked at Margaret over breakfast and said, "If one of us goes first, I don't want the other dealing with court nonsense. Let's get this sorted."

A solicitor gave them a dizzying explanation of discretionary trusts and tax wrappers. The price tag: **£1,800**. They left more confused than when they arrived. Margaret whispered on the drive home, "Alan, we don't need all that, do we?"

They sat down at their dining table — covered in a floral cloth and stacks of printed guidance from gov.uk — and realised all they needed was a **basic family trust**. Alan would act as trustee, Margaret would be successor, and the grandchildren would inherit.

The process felt surprisingly human. At the Land Registry office, the clerk smiled and said, "Lots of people your age do this themselves now." They paid **£40**, updated their title, and went home.

The moment the confirmation letter arrived, Alan tapped the paper with satisfaction. "That's our legacy secured," he said. Margaret nodded, tears in her eyes. Total spend? About **£350**. Savings? More than a month's pension.

UK Story 3 – The Divorced Dad in Glasgow

Kevin, fifty, worked shifts in a Glasgow factory. His teenage daughter, Isla, lived with him most of the time. His greatest fear was that if he died, Isla's mother (his ex-wife) might gain control over the house.

A solicitor quoted him **£2,200** for a discretionary trust. Kevin thought, *That's nearly the cost of Isla's braces.* He considered giving up — but then he discovered something called a **bare trust**. Simple. Direct. Just passing the property to Isla when she turned eighteen.

He drafted it himself, appointed his brother as successor trustee, and filed the TR1 form. The only hiccup came later: his insurance policy still listed him personally, not "Kevin as Trustee." When the insurer called to update renewal, Kevin caught the mistake. "Good spot," the rep said, "We'll adjust that."

Cost: **£360**. Peace of mind: priceless. Kevin said later, "Now I know if anything happens, my girl won't have to fight anyone for her home."

US Story 1 – The Couple in Ohio

Linda and Mark had a tidy two-story home outside Columbus. With both kids in their twenties, they were thinking about the future. Probate horror stories from friends haunted them. One night, Linda asked Mark, "What if we make it easy for the kids? No courts. No lawyers."

They went to a local attorney for advice. The quote? **$3,500** for a revocable trust. "That's ridiculous," Mark muttered in the car park.

So they tried a DIY path. They bought a $75 trust template, filled it in, and went to a notary ($20). Next, they recorded a quitclaim deed transferring the house to the trust at the County Recorder's office. Fee: **$92**.

Linda remembers the clerk leaning in and saying, "We see this more and more — people doing it themselves." They made three copies of the documents: one at home, one in a safe deposit box, and one online.

Total cost? **$250**. "For less than what we spend on a weekend getaway, we saved the kids years of hassle," Linda said.

US Story 2 – The Single Father in Texas

Raymond lived in Houston with two teenagers. His modest ranch house had a small mortgage. When a lawyer quoted him **$4,200** for a trust, Raymond laughed. "That's one semester of college tuition."

He called his lender first. The rep reassured him: "As long as you're still trustee, we don't care." That green light gave him courage. He bought a $50 trust kit, named himself trustee, his sister as successor, and his kids as beneficiaries.

He went to a local notary ($10), then walked into the Harris County Clerk's office with his deed. The staff patiently explained which boxes to tick. Filing fee: **$112**.

Raymond's only mistake was forgetting to update his homeowners' insurance. Two months later, he called in and fixed it at no cost. His spend? **$180**. He told me, "I thought this was lawyer stuff. Turns out it's just paperwork if you pay attention."

US Story 3 – The Retired Teacher in California

Susan, a retired teacher in Sacramento, adored her nieces. With no children of her own, she wanted them to inherit her bungalow smoothly. When she asked about a trust, the estate lawyer pitched a "full estate package" for **$5,000**. Susan nearly fainted.

She opted for DIY. She paid $50 for a trust deed template, $25 for a mobile notary, and **$80** at the county recorder's office. Before mailing the grant deed, she rang the office: "I just want to be sure I've filled this right." The clerk kindly confirmed each detail.

Susan admitted later: "The hardest part was convincing myself I could do it. But once the recorder sent me confirmation, I felt free."

Her nieces now have both the house and an education fund — paid for with the $5,000 Susan didn't hand over to a lawyer.

Big Lessons from These Stories

1. Ordinary people — single parents, retirees, couples — all handled trusts successfully without lawyers.
2. The **DIY cost ranged from £350–£380 in the UK and $150–$250 in the US.**
3. Mistakes happened (insurance updates, forgetting successors), but were easy to fix.

4. Families gained more than money: they gained peace of mind, control, and confidence.

Chapter 9 – Selling, Refinancing, and Life After the Trust

So, you've gone through all the paperwork, set up your trust, and tucked your house into it neatly. You breathe a sigh of relief, maybe even pat yourself on the back — job well done. But now what? Life doesn't freeze the day you file a deed or sign a trust document. Families grow, kids move out, marriages shift, mortgages end, and sometimes, the house you thought you'd never leave suddenly needs to be sold or refinanced.

This chapter tackles the big question: **what happens after the trust is in place?** Can you sell? Can you refinance? Can you change things later? Absolutely — but there are steps, conditions, and small traps to avoid. Let's walk through it carefully, one situation at a time.

Selling Your Home While It's in a Trust

Here's the deal: having your property in a trust does not lock it away forever. People often think a trust is a cage — it's not. Think of it more like a wrapper. You still have the keys, but when you sell, the wrapper has to move with you or be undone first.

- **In the UK**: If you're both trustee and beneficiary (say you're the parent and your kids are the beneficiaries), you can sell the property. But the sale proceeds usually go into the trust account. That means when the sale completes, instead of the cheque being cut to "Mr. John

Smith," it will say "John Smith as Trustee of the Smith Family Trust." From there, you can use the funds to buy another property into the trust or distribute according to trust rules.

- **In the US**: Similar story. If it's a **revocable living trust** and you're the trustee, you can sell the property almost as though it were still in your name. Title companies see this all the time. The sale deed will list you as "Jane Doe, Trustee of the Doe Family Trust." The proceeds flow back into the trust, not you personally — though if you're both trustee and beneficiary, you still control it.

Common worry: "But will buyers freak out if the house is in a trust?" Answer: not at all. In both the UK and US, it's standard practice. Title companies, conveyancers, and registrars handle it every week.

Case Example – Selling in the UK

Harriet, a widowed grandmother in Surrey, had placed her cottage into a bare trust with her three grandchildren as beneficiaries. Years later, she decided to downsize. The estate agent asked, "Is this in your name?" Harriet proudly said, "It's in my family trust." For a moment, the agent frowned — but when Harriet's conveyancer received the trust deed, it was a non-issue. The only hiccup was that the buyer's solicitor asked for a copy of the trust document. Harriet provided it, and the sale went through smoothly.

Her cottage sold for £380,000. The proceeds went into the trust account, and Harriet used £280,000 to purchase a smaller flat — also placed into the trust. Cost? Just the usual Land Registry fee. No solicitor fee, because she reused the steps she'd learned years earlier.

Case Example – Selling in the US

Thomas and Rachel in Arizona had placed their desert ranch into a revocable trust. When they decided to move to Florida to be closer to their kids, they were nervous: "Will the buyers refuse a trust title?" Their realtor laughed: "Half my sales are from trusts these days."

The deed was signed: "Thomas and Rachel Jones, Trustees of the Jones Family Trust." At closing, the cheque was written to the trust. They immediately rolled the funds into a Florida condo, retitling it under the same trust. Smooth as silk.

Their comment later: "We were scared of nothing. The trust moved with us like luggage on a plane."

Refinancing Your Home in a Trust

This part gets slightly trickier. Lenders can be picky — some dislike the word "trust," fearing legal tangles. But let's separate UK and US.

- **UK**: If your property has a mortgage, you generally need **lender consent** before transferring it into a trust. Most big banks (Santander, Nationwide, Barclays) will allow it if you remain trustee. When refinancing, the bank may ask you to temporarily transfer the title back into your own name, then re-deed it into the trust after. It sounds messy, but it's routine. Costs are limited to admin and small registry fees.
- **US**: With a **revocable trust**, lenders are usually fine — Fannie Mae and Freddie Mac (the big secondary mortgage buyers) both approve lending on trust-held

properties if the borrower is trustee and beneficiary. However, like the UK, some banks ask you to deed the property out of the trust, refinance, then place it back in. Annoying? Yes. Impossible? No.

Practical tip: Always keep your trust deed and certificate ready. Banks will ask for it. Don't panic when they do.

Case Example – Refinancing in the UK

David in Liverpool put his terraced house into trust with his two children as beneficiaries. When interest rates dipped, he applied for a new mortgage. The lender said, "We'll need the property out of the trust during the refinance." For three weeks, the house was legally back in David's personal name. Once the new loan funded, he re-registered the title into the trust. Cost? £40 at the Land Registry each time. Savings on his monthly payment? £220. Worth it.

Case Example – Refinancing in the US

Maria, a nurse in California, had her home in a living trust. She wanted to refinance for a lower rate. The lender asked for a copy of the trust and proof that it was revocable (meaning Maria still controlled it). The underwriter checked the documents, approved the loan, and the trust stayed intact the whole time. Maria avoided the "in-and-out" shuffle.

Her words: "It felt no different than refinancing normally. Just one extra document."

Life After the Trust: Everyday Realities

Once the trust is set up, daily life doesn't change much. You still live in the house, pay your bills, mow the lawn, argue about bins, and complain about property taxes. But here are the subtle differences you'll notice over time:

1. **Insurance**: Your home insurance should list the trust as an interested party. Otherwise, if you file a claim, the insurance cheque could come in your personal name and create confusion. Call your insurer, say: "Please add the XYZ Family Trust as additional insured." Takes five minutes.
2. **Taxes**: In both the UK and US, if it's a revocable or bare trust, your tax situation doesn't change. You still report property taxes the same way. No extra tax bills sneak up.
3. **Inheritance process**: The biggest difference shows when someone dies. The house skips probate. In the UK, that saves months of waiting. In the US, it can save a year of court headaches and thousands in legal fees.
4. **Flexibility**: You can still buy, sell, refinance, or even take the house out of the trust entirely if you change your mind. Revocable trusts are not handcuffs.

Biggest Surprises Homeowners Report

- They feared the trust would complicate their life — but it actually simplified it.
- They expected buyers or lenders to push back — but most didn't care.
- They thought insurance would be a nightmare — but it was a phone call.
- They imagined huge tax changes — but saw none.

Life After Trust Stories

UK – Margaret's Quiet Relief
Margaret, seventy-five, said the real comfort came not in the paperwork, but in her sleep. "I don't wake up at night worrying anymore. The flat is sorted for the kids. That's enough for me."

US – Jason's Family Reunion
Jason, a widower in Florida, said his children stopped arguing once the trust was set up. "No one debates what happens to the house now. It's all in writing. The trust removed the drama before it started."

Key Takeaways from Chapter 9

- Selling is straightforward: the trust sells, not you personally, but the money stays in your hands if you're trustee and beneficiary.
- Refinancing may require short-term adjustments, but it's legal and normal.
- Everyday life doesn't change much — except for the peace of mind.
- Your heirs avoid probate. That's the real payoff.

Chapter 10 – Advanced Trust Tweaks for Special Cases

By now, you've got the core process down. You understand what a trust is, why it works, and how to get your property into one without breaking the bank. You even know what happens after the fact — selling, refinancing, living your daily life.

But real life isn't always neat. Families are complicated. Houses aren't always just "homes" — sometimes they're rentals, sometimes they're joint with a new partner, sometimes they're vacation homes in another state or county. And sometimes, the people you want to inherit aren't just kids — maybe it's stepchildren, nieces, or a second spouse you want protected.

This is where the **tweaks** come in. The trust framework is simple, but you can tailor it like a suit. In this chapter, we'll walk through **special cases** where small adjustments make a huge difference.

Blended Families and Second Marriages

Let's face it — not every family looks like the picture on a Christmas card. Divorce, remarriage, stepkids, and half-siblings are part of modern life. And that's exactly where trusts shine, because a trust lets you decide who gets what, without courts or default laws interfering.

- **In the UK**: Say Peter remarries after his wife's death. He owns a home in Birmingham worth £450,000. He wants his new wife, Laura, to be able to live there if he dies first — but ultimately, he wants the property to go to his two children from his first marriage. A simple will might not be enough (Laura could challenge it). But a **life interest trust** solves this neatly. Laura has the right to live in the house for her lifetime, but when she passes away, the property automatically goes to Peter's children. No arguments, no court fights.

- **In the US**: Similar story. John in Ohio remarries and wants his second wife to stay in their house until her death — but then the property should go to his son from his first marriage. A **QTIP trust (Qualified Terminable Interest Property trust)** allows exactly that. Wife is secure, but the inheritance is locked in for the child.

The beauty of these setups? They prevent the classic "Cinderella problem," where stepchildren get cut out or new spouses lose their homes.

Case Example – UK Blended Family

Christine had two children from her first marriage. When she remarried, she wanted her second husband to be cared for, but also to guarantee her kids inherited. She used a trust that let her husband live in the house rent-free for life, but barred him from selling it. When he passed, the trust instructed that the property title move to her children. The result? No bickering, no courts, no solicitor fees. Just peace.

Case Example – US Blended Family

Mark, a retired teacher in California, remarried at 65. His new wife had her own children, and his kids were grown. To avoid a family feud, he placed his house into a revocable trust with a special clause: if he died first, his wife could live in the house as long as she wished, but when she no longer lived there, his kids would inherit. That clause prevented his wife's children from ever claiming the property. Everyone knew the rules upfront.

Rental Properties in a Trust

What if your property isn't your home, but a rental? Good news — you can place rental properties into a trust just like your primary residence. But here's where the tweaks matter.

- **UK Rentals**: If you hold a buy-to-let under a trust, rental income is still taxable in your name if it's a bare or simple trust. That means no tax break — but also no new paperwork. If you want the rental income to flow directly to beneficiaries (say, your adult children), you can set up a discretionary trust. The downside: more complicated tax reporting.
- **US Rentals**: A rental home in a revocable living trust works fine. You still report income on your personal return. But if you want asset protection (to shield yourself from tenant lawsuits), consider pairing the trust with an LLC. Some families place the LLC into the trust, making the trust the owner of the company that owns the rental. Double protection, same peace of mind.

Case Example – UK Rental Owner

Omar in London had two flats he rented to students. He put both into his family trust. The rents kept flowing into his account because it was a bare trust, so no new HMRC headaches. But the real win? When Omar died, the trust avoided probate, and his children immediately started receiving the rent checks. His daughter called it "the smoothest handover of income I've ever seen."

Case Example – US Rental Owner

Lydia in Texas had a duplex she rented. To avoid court delays for her kids, she placed it in a living trust. But she added one smart tweak: she made the trust the sole owner of her LLC, which technically held the duplex. If a tenant sued, they had to sue the LLC, not her or her kids. And when Lydia passed, the LLC shares passed straight through the trust to her children — no probate, no fuss.

Vacation Homes and Out-of-State Property

Another special case: second homes or property in another state (for US readers) or another part of the UK (say, Scotland).

- **In the UK**: If you own property in Scotland but live in England, probate can get complicated because of different legal systems. A trust covering both avoids multiple probate processes.
- **In the US**: If you live in New York but have a cabin in Vermont and a condo in Florida, your heirs would face **ancillary probate** in each state. With a trust, all those properties pass seamlessly under one umbrella. That alone can save thousands in legal fees.

Case Example – US Vacation Home

Nancy, a Boston resident, had a holiday condo in Florida. When she died, her kids would have had to go through Massachusetts probate **and** Florida probate. Instead, she titled both her Massachusetts home and Florida condo into one trust. Result: single streamlined inheritance. Her kids said later: "It felt like she was still taking care of us."

Protecting Vulnerable Beneficiaries

What if your intended heir isn't fully independent? Maybe they're too young, or maybe they struggle with addiction, disability, or financial recklessness. Handing them a property directly could be disastrous.

This is where **protective or discretionary trusts** are useful.

- **In the UK**: You can appoint trustees (including yourself while alive) to manage property for vulnerable beneficiaries. That way, a 19-year-old doesn't suddenly own a house they can't maintain. Trustees can decide when and how the property is used.
- **In the US**: A **special needs trust** allows you to leave a house to a disabled child without cutting off their government benefits. Or you can create restrictions that prevent a reckless heir from selling the home the day they inherit it.

Case Example – Protecting a Son in the UK

Helen had a son, James, who struggled with gambling. She feared that if he inherited her home outright, he'd sell it immediately. Instead, she used a discretionary trust. The trustees (including Helen's brother) had control over the property. James could live there, but he couldn't sell it without trustee approval. Helen's peace of mind was worth every minute of paperwork.

Case Example – Protecting a Daughter in the US

Robert had a daughter with a developmental disability. If she inherited property directly, she could lose Medicaid eligibility. He set up a special needs trust that owned the family home. His daughter lived there, with expenses paid from the trust. She never lost her benefits, and she never risked being homeless.

Quick Tweaks That Save Families Headaches

Here are the most common tweaks people make:

1. **Life interest trusts** (UK) or **QTIP trusts** (US) for second marriages.
2. **Discretionary trusts** for adult children who aren't ready for full control.
3. **Special needs trusts** for disabled heirs.
4. **LLC plus trust combo** for rental properties (US).
5. **Cross-border coverage** for multiple properties in different states or UK regions.

Key Takeaways from Chapter 10

- Trusts are flexible — you don't need a "perfect" nuclear family for them to work.
- Small tweaks like life interest provisions or LLC layering make trusts fit complex lives.

- Blended families, rentals, vacation homes, and vulnerable heirs all benefit from trust customization.
- The same core idea applies: the trust keeps control with you and prevents court headaches for your loved ones.

Special Cases at a Glance

Blended Families	**USE A** Life interest trust for spouse
Vacation Homes	**CONSIDER A(N)** LLC plus trust
Vulnerable Heirs	**AVOID** Ancillary probate

Chapter 11 – Frequently Asked Questions Simplified

Even when the paperwork is explained step by step, people still worry about the details. This section clears the fog by answering the exact questions homeowners in the **UK** and **US** ask most often. To make it easier, I've split the FAQs into two parts — one tailored to the UK system, and one for the US.

UK Homeowners: Top 10 FAQs

1. Do I still own my home after moving it into a trust?
Yes, you remain the beneficial owner. The legal title goes into the name of the trustee (which can be you), but you control it. The main difference is that when you pass away, the property doesn't go through probate.

2. Will I need my lender's permission if I still have a mortgage?
Yes. UK lenders require consent before you transfer a mortgaged property into a trust. Most approve it as long as your payments remain current. Sometimes they'll charge a small administration fee.

3. Does it save me inheritance tax?
Not automatically. A simple living trust avoids probate but does not reduce inheritance tax on its own. However, specific types of trusts, such as discretionary or life interest trusts, can help with inheritance planning.

4. What happens to capital gains tax if I sell?
If the property is your main home, your principal private residence relief still applies. That means no capital gains tax on

the sale. For second homes or rental properties, the normal capital gains rules apply.

5. Can I refinance my mortgage once the house is in a trust?
Yes, but some lenders prefer the property to be transferred back into your individual name temporarily for refinancing. Once done, you can move it back into the trust.

6. Do I need more than one trustee?
Not necessarily. You can be the sole trustee. However, it's smart to name at least one successor trustee who can take over if you die or lose capacity.

7. Can my children inherit through the trust even if they are minors?
Yes. The trust holds the property until they reach adulthood (usually 18 in England and Wales, 16 in Scotland). You can specify conditions, such as holding until they are 21 or 25.

8. Do I still need a will?
Yes, ideally a simple "backup" will. It can cover assets you forget to move into the trust and give instructions for personal effects.

9. Does my insurance need updating?
Yes. You should inform your home insurance provider that the legal title is in the name of the trustee. Otherwise, a claim could be disputed.

10. What's the biggest mistake people make in the UK?
The top mistake is setting up a trust but failing to register the transfer with HM Land Registry. Without updating the official records, the trust doesn't legally own the property.

US Homeowners: Top 10 FAQs

1. Do I still control my home once it's in a trust?
Yes. With a revocable living trust, you are usually both trustee and beneficiary while alive. You control the property exactly as before.

2. Does putting my home into a trust trigger the "due on sale" clause in my mortgage?
No. Federal law (Garn–St. Germain Act of 1982) protects homeowners who transfer their property into their own revocable trust. The bank cannot call the loan due.

3. Will I save on estate taxes?
No. A living trust avoids probate but doesn't reduce estate tax. For tax savings, you'd need more complex planning, such as irrevocable trusts or marital trusts.

4. What happens when I sell my home from the trust?
You can sell it just like before. The only change is that the deed will be signed by you in your capacity as trustee. Capital gains exclusions for primary residences still apply.

5. Can I refinance a house in a trust?
Yes, but some lenders will ask you to temporarily deed it back to your name for the refinance process. Once the loan closes, you can put it back into the trust.

6. Can my minor children be beneficiaries?
Yes. The trust holds the property until they reach an age you set, such as 18, 21, or 25. This protects against children inheriting too young.

7. Do I still need a will if I have a trust?
Yes. You should create a "pour-over will." This acts as a safety

net, automatically moving any assets not titled in the trust into it when you die.

8. Is a trust public record?
No. Unlike a will, which becomes public once probated, a living trust remains private. Only the deed showing the trustee's name is public. The details of beneficiaries remain confidential.

9. What's the biggest mistake people make in the US?
Two common ones: forgetting to re-title the deed into the trust, and not updating homeowners' insurance. Both errors leave the trust incomplete and may cause disputes.

10. Can I remove my property from the trust later?
Yes. A revocable living trust is designed to be flexible. You can transfer the property back into your name or sell it outright.

Key Takeaways from Chapter 11

- UK and US processes share similarities but differ in lender rules, tax laws, and beneficiary ages.
- You don't lose control of your property by placing it into a trust.
- Insurance updates, lender communication, and successor trustee naming are essential in both countries.
- A will is still useful as a backup in every case.
- Most mistakes come down to paperwork left unfinished.

Chapter 12 – UK Templates and Tools

When it comes to property trusts, the paperwork often feels scarier than it actually is. The truth? Most of it comes down to writing a handful of clear letters and filling out standard forms. This chapter gives you **ready-made templates** for the exact documents you'll need. Just plug in your name, address, and property details — and you're set.

---

1. Letter to Mortgage Lender (Request for Consent)

```
[Your Full Name]
[Your Address]
[Postcode]

[Date]

Mortgage Servicing Department
[Bank/Lender Name]
[Bank Address]

Re: Request for Consent to Transfer Property into a
Trust
Account No: [Mortgage Account Number]
Property Address: [Property Address]

Dear Sir/Madam,

I am writing to request your consent to transfer the
legal title of my property into a family trust. I
confirm that I will remain fully responsible for the
existing mortgage obligations, and no terms of
repayment will be affected.

The trust arrangement is for estate planning
purposes only, and the property will continue to be
```

occupied as my primary residence. Please advise if
any specific forms or fees are required to complete
this transfer with your records.

Thank you for your assistance.

Yours sincerely,
[Signature]
[Printed Name]

---

2. Cover Letter to HM Land Registry (Submitting TR1 and AP1)

[Your Full Name]
[Your Address]
[Postcode]

[Date]

HM Land Registry
Citizen Centre
PO Box 74
Gloucester GL14 9BB

Dear Sir/Madam,

Re: Application to Register Transfer of Property
into Trust
Property Address: [Property Address]
Title Number: [Land Registry Title Number]

Please find enclosed the following:

- Completed TR1 Transfer Form
- Completed AP1 Application Form
- Certified copy of Trust Deed
- Proof of ID (Form ID1)
- Payment of Land Registry fee [£ amount]

I kindly request registration of the above property
into [Name of Trust].

Yours faithfully,
[Signature]

[Printed Name]

---

3. Letter to Home Insurance Provider

[Your Full Name]
[Your Address]
[Postcode]

[Date]

[Insurance Company Name]
[Insurance Company Address]

Dear Sir/Madam,

Re: Update of Insurance Policy for Property in Trust
Policy Number: [Policy Number]
Property Address: [Property Address]

I am writing to notify you that the legal title of
the above property has been transferred into [Name
of Trust]. I remain the beneficial owner and
occupant of the property.

Please update your records to reflect that the
trustee(s) of the trust now hold the legal title.
Kindly confirm that this does not affect the
coverage or validity of my policy.

Yours sincerely,
[Signature]
[Printed Name]

---

4. Sample Trust Deeds

1. Standard Family Home Trust Deed

TRUST DEED

This Trust Deed is made on [Date].

Between:
[Full Name of Settlor], of [Address] ("the Settlor")

and
[Full Name of Trustee(s)], of [Address(es)] ("the Trustee(s)")

1. The Settlor transfers the property known as [Property Address] and registered under Title Number [Title Number] into this Trust.

2. The Trustee(s) shall hold the property on trust for the Beneficiaries:
   - [List full names of Beneficiaries].

3. The Trustee(s) may sell, lease, or manage the property for the benefit of the Beneficiaries.

4. The Settlor may occupy the property during their lifetime.

Signed:
_____ (Settlor)
_____ (Trustee)

Witness:
Name: _____
Address: _____
Signature: _____
Date: _____

2. Family Home Trust with Mortgage (UK)

ADDITIONAL CLAUSE:

The Trustee(s) acknowledge that the property remains subject to the existing mortgage with [Lender's Name]. The Settlor and Trustee(s) agree to remain bound by the terms of the mortgage and confirm that lender's consent has been obtained.

(Insert this clause into the Standard Trust Deed before signing.)

3. Trust with Replacement Trustee (UK)

ADDITIONAL CLAUSE:

If [Name of Original Trustee] dies, resigns, or is
unable to act, then [Name of Replacement Trustee]
shall automatically become Trustee in their place.

4. Trust with Children as Sole Beneficiaries (UK)

BENEFICIARY CLAUSE:

The Trustee(s) shall hold the property solely for
the benefit of the following children:
[List full names and dates of birth].

The property shall be managed until each child
attains the age of 21, at which time the Trustee(s)
may transfer legal ownership as directed by this
Trust.

Model UK Trust Deed (Complete with All Clauses)

TRUST DEED

THIS TRUST DEED is made on [Date].

BETWEEN:

(1) [Full Name of Settlor], of [Settlor's Address]
("the Settlor"); and
(2) [Full Name(s) of Trustee(s)], of [Trustee(s)'
Address(es)] ("the Trustee(s)").

RECITALS:

A. The Settlor is the registered proprietor of the property known as [Property Address] and registered under Title Number [Title Number].
B. The Settlor wishes to transfer the property into trust for the benefit of the Beneficiaries named below.
C. The Settlor intends this Trust to take effect immediately and acknowledges that it may continue beyond their lifetime.

OPERATIVE PROVISIONS:

1. TRANSFER OF PROPERTY
The Settlor hereby transfers the property described above into this Trust to be held by the Trustee(s) upon the trusts and subject to the powers and provisions contained in this Deed.

2. BENEFICIARIES
The Beneficiaries of this Trust are:
[List full names of Beneficiaries and their relationship to Settlor].
Where Beneficiaries are minor children, the Trustee(s) shall hold the property for their benefit until they each attain the age of 21 years.

3. OCCUPATION RIGHTS
The Settlor may occupy and use the property during their lifetime, provided that mortgage obligations and property expenses are met.

4. MORTGAGE CLAUSE
Where the property is subject to a mortgage with [Lender's Name], the property shall remain subject to that mortgage. The Trustee(s) and Settlor agree to observe the terms of the mortgage and confirm that lender's consent has been obtained.

5. TRUSTEE POWERS
The Trustee(s) shall have the following powers:
- To sell, lease, or mortgage the property, provided such actions benefit the Beneficiaries.
- To insure, maintain, and repair the property.
- To invest any proceeds of sale for the benefit of the Beneficiaries.

6. SUCCESSOR TRUSTEE
If any Trustee dies, resigns, or is unable to act,
then [Name of Replacement Trustee] shall
automatically become Trustee in their place.

7. TRUSTEE LIABILITY
No Trustee shall be liable for any loss to the Trust
unless caused by their own fraud or deliberate
wrongdoing.

8. REVOCATION
This Trust may be revoked by the Settlor during
their lifetime by written notice to the Trustee(s).
If not revoked, it shall continue after the
Settlor's death.

IN WITNESS WHEREOF this Deed has been executed and
delivered as a deed on the date first above written.

Signed as a Deed by:
_____ (Settlor)

In the presence of:
Witness Name: _____
Address: _____
Signature: _____

Signed as a Deed by:
_____ (Trustee)

In the presence of:
Witness Name: _____
Address: _____
Signature: _____

5. Checklist: UK Trust Transfer Documents

- Trust Deed (signed, dated, witnessed)
- TR1 Transfer Form
- AP1 Application Form
- ID1 Identity Verification Form

- Lender's consent letter (if mortgaged)
- Updated home insurance policy
- Land Registry fee payment

Chapter 13 – US Templates and Tools

1. Letter to Mortgage Lender (Notification)

```
[Your Full Name]
[Your Address]
[City, State, ZIP]

[Date]

Mortgage Servicing Department
[Bank/Lender Name]
[Bank Address]

Re: Transfer of Property into Revocable Living Trust
Loan Number: [Loan Number]
Property Address: [Property Address]

Dear Sir/Madam,

This letter is to inform you that I have transferred
the above property into the [Name of Trust], dated
[Date]. This is a revocable living trust in which I
am both the trustee and the beneficiary.

This transfer does not affect my obligations under
the mortgage. Payments will continue as usual.
Please update your records to reflect that the
property is now held in trust.

Sincerely,
[Signature]
[Printed Name]
```

2. Letter to County Recorder (Deed Filing Cover Note)

```
[Your Full Name]
[Your Address]
```

[City, State, ZIP]

[Date]

[County Recorder's Office]
[Recorder Address]

Dear Clerk,

Re: Recording of Trust Transfer Deed
Property Address: [Property Address]

Please find enclosed:

- Original Trust Transfer Deed
- Copy of Trust Certificate (or full Trust
Agreement, if required)
- Payment of recording fee [$ amount]

Kindly record the enclosed deed and return the
stamped copy to me at the above address.

Thank you for your assistance.

Sincerely,
[Signature]
[Printed Name]

---

3. Letter to Home Insurance Provider

[Your Full Name]
[Your Address]
[City, State, ZIP]

[Date]

[Insurance Company Name]
[Insurance Company Address]

Dear Sir/Madam,

Re: Update of Insurance Policy for Property in Trust
Policy Number: [Policy Number]
Property Address: [Property Address]

I am writing to advise that the property listed above has been transferred into the [Name of Trust]. I remain the trustee and beneficiary of the trust.

Please update your records accordingly and confirm that the coverage remains active and unaffected.

Sincerely,
[Signature]
[Printed Name]

---

4. Sample Trust Deeds

1. Standard Revocable Living Trust Deed

DECLARATION OF TRUST

This Trust Agreement is made on [Date].

Between:
[Full Name of Grantor/Settlor], of [Address] ("the Grantor")

and
[Full Name of Trustee(s)], of [Address(es)] ("the Trustee(s)")

1. The Grantor transfers the property located at [Property Address] into this Trust.

2. The Trustee(s) shall hold the property for the use and benefit of the Beneficiaries:
    - [List full names of Beneficiaries].

3. The Grantor reserves the right to live in and use the property during their lifetime.

4. This Trust is revocable. The Grantor may amend or terminate it at any time.

Signed:
_____ (Grantor)

_____ (Trustee)

Witness/Notary Public:
Name: _____
Address: _____
Signature: _____
Date: _____

2. Trust Deed with Mortgage (US)

ADDITIONAL CLAUSE:

The property remains subject to the existing
mortgage with [Lender's Name]. The Grantor confirms
that mortgage payments shall continue unchanged, and
lender notification has been provided.

3. Trust with Replacement Trustee (US)

SUCCESSOR TRUSTEE CLAUSE:

If [Name of Original Trustee] is unable or unwilling
to serve, then [Name of Successor Trustee] shall act
with full authority under this Trust.

4. Trust with Children as Sole Beneficiaries (US)

BENEFICIARY CLAUSE:

The Trustee(s) shall hold the property solely for
the benefit of the following children:
[List full names and dates of birth].

The Trustee(s) shall manage the property until each
child reaches age 21, unless oth

Model US Trust Deed (Complete with All Clauses)

DECLARATION OF TRUST

THIS TRUST AGREEMENT is made on [Date].

BETWEEN:

(1) [Full Name of Grantor/Settlor], of [Settlor's Address] ("the Grantor"); and
(2) [Full Name(s) of Trustee(s)], of [Trustee(s)' Address(es)] ("the Trustee(s)").

RECITALS:

A. The Grantor is the owner of the property located at [Property Address].
B. The Grantor desires to establish a revocable living trust to hold and manage said property for the benefit of the Beneficiaries.
C. The Grantor may amend or revoke this Trust during their lifetime.

OPERATIVE PROVISIONS:

1. TRANSFER OF PROPERTY
The Grantor hereby transfers and assigns to the Trustee(s) the property located at [Property Address] to be held, administered, and distributed in accordance with this Trust.

2. BENEFICIARIES
The Beneficiaries of this Trust are:
[List full names of Beneficiaries].
Where Beneficiaries are minor children, the Trustee(s) shall manage the property until each child reaches the age of 21, or such other age as may be specified in a written amendment.

3. RESERVATION OF USE
The Grantor reserves the right to live in and use the property during their lifetime.

4. MORTGAGE CLAUSE
The Grantor acknowledges that the property romains subject to a mortgage with [Lender's Name]. The Grantor agrees to continue all obligations under

97

said mortgage. Lender notification has been
provided.

5. TRUSTEE POWERS
The Trustee(s) shall have authority:
- To sell, lease, or mortgage the property.
- To reinvest any proceeds of sale for the benefit
of the Beneficiaries.
- To insure and maintain the property.

6. SUCCESSOR TRUSTEE
If [Name of Original Trustee] is unwilling or unable
to act, then [Name of Successor Trustee] shall serve
as Trustee with full authority.

7. TRUSTEE LIABILITY
No Trustee shall be liable for any loss to the Trust
unless caused by their own fraud or willful
misconduct.

8. REVOCATION OR AMENDMENT
This Trust is revocable. The Grantor may revoke or
amend this Trust by a signed writing delivered to
the Trustee(s) during their lifetime.

EXECUTION:

_____ (Grantor/Settlor)
Date: _____

_____ (Trustee)
Date: _____

STATE OF [State], COUNTY OF [County]

On this ___ day of [Month, Year], before me, the
undersigned Notary Public, personally appeared
[Name(s)], personally known to me or proven to me on
satisfactory evidence to be the person(s) whose
name(s) are subscribed to this instrument, and
acknowledged that they executed the same.

IN WITNESS WHEREOF, I have hereunto set my hand and
official seal.

_____

5. Checklist: US Trust Transfer Documents

- Trust Transfer Deed (quitclaim deed or warranty deed into trust)
- Certificate of Trust (or full trust)
- Notarization of deed
- County recorder filing fee
- Lender notification letter (if mortgaged)
- Updated insurance policy

Key Takeaway of Chapter 12

With these templates and checklists, you don't need to overthink the process. The heavy lifting is already done — all that's left is to fill in your details, keep copies, and send them to the right offices.

References

UK

HM Land Registry (2023). *Registered Titles: Whole Transfer (Form TR1)*. Available at: https://www.gov.uk/government/publications/registered-titles-whole-transfer-tr1 (Accessed: 21 August 2025).

HM Land Registry (2023). *Change the Register (Form AP1)*. Available at: https://www.gov.uk/government/publications/change-the-register-ap1 (Accessed: 21 August 2025).

HM Land Registry (2023). *How to Complete Form TR1 (Guidance Notes)*. Available at: https://assets.publishing.service.gov.uk/media/65afbf6870218e000cb41f89/TR1__2023-08-29_ct.pdf (Accessed: 21 August 2025).

HM Land Registry (2023). *How to Complete AP1 Form (Video Guide)*. Available at: https://www.youtube.com/watch?v=QMFQaGZYgBA (Accessed: 21 August 2025).

HM Land Registry (2023). *Common Mistakes to Avoid in Applications (Video)*. Available at: https://www.youtube.com/watch?v=i79AMqCHY1I (Accessed: 21 August 2025).

US

Los Angeles County Registrar-Recorder (2023). *Recording Requirements*. Available at: https://www.lavote.gov/home/recorder/property-document-recording/recording-requirements (Accessed: 21 August 2025).

San Diego County Assessor/Recorder/Clerk (2023). *Recording Requirements*. Available at: https://www.sdarcc.gov/content/arcc/home/divisions/recorder-clerk/recording.html (Accessed: 21 August 2025).

Orange County Clerk-Recorder (2023). *Property Document Recording Services*. Available at: https://ocrecorder.com/recorder-services/property-documentsdocument-recording-services (Accessed: 21 August 2025).

Ventura County Clerk-Recorder (2023). *General Recording Requirements*. Available at: https://clerkrecorder.venturacounty.gov/county-recorder/county-recorder/official-records/general-recording-requirements/ (Accessed: 21 August 2025).

Harris County Clerk's Office (2023). *Recording Requirements*. Available at: https://www.cclerk.hctx.net/RecordingRequirements.aspx (Accessed: 21 August 2025).

Investopedia (2023). *Deed of Reconveyance*. Available at: https://www.investopedia.com/terms/d/deed-of-reconveyance.asp (Accessed: 21 August 2025).

www.ingramcontent.com/pod-product-compliance
Lightning Source LLC
LaVergne TN
LVHW051700080426
835511LV00017B/2653